Snakes

BACKYARD WILDLIFE

Snakes

by Emily Green

BELLWETHER MEDIA • MINNEAPOLIS, MN

BLASTOFF!
READERS

Note to Librarians, Teachers, and Parents:

Blastoff! Readers are carefully developed by literacy experts and combine standards-based content with developmentally appropriate text.

Level 1 provides the most support through repetition of high-frequency words, light text, predictable sentence patterns, and strong visual support.

Level 2 offers early readers a bit more challenge through varied simple sentences, increased text load, and less repetition of high-frequency words.

Level 3 advances early-fluent readers toward fluency through increased text and concept load, less reliance on visuals, longer sentences, and more literary language.

Level 4 builds reading stamina by providing more text per page, increased use of punctuation, greater variation in sentence patterns, and increasingly challenging vocabulary.

Level 5 encourages children to move from "learning to read" to "reading to learn" by providing even more text, varied writing styles, and less familiar topics.

Whichever book is right for your reader, Blastoff! Readers are the perfect books to build confidence and encourage a love of reading that will last a lifetime!

This edition first published in 2011 by Bellwether Media, Inc.

No part of this publication may be reproduced in whole or in part without written permission of the publisher. For information regarding permission, write to Bellwether Media, Inc., Attention: Permissions Department, 5357 Penn Avenue South, Minneapolis, MN 55419.

Library of Congress Cataloging-in-Publication Data
Green, Emily K., 1966–
Snakes / by Emily Green.
    p. cm. – (Blastoff! readers. Backyard wildlife)
Summary: "Developed by literacy experts for students in kindergarten through grade three, this book introduces snakes to young readers through leveled text and related photos"–Provided by publisher.
Includes bibliographical references and index.
ISBN 978-1-60014-446-2 (hardcover : alk. paper)
1. Snakes–Juvenile literature. I. Title.
QL666.O6G683 2010
597.96–dc22   2010010685

Printed in the United States of America, North Mankato, MN.
080110   1162

Contents

Snakes are animals with long bodies. They come in many sizes.

Snakes have **scales** on their skin. Snakes **shed** their skin as they grow.

Snakes come in different colors. Most have stripes, spots, or other **patterns** on their scales.

Some snakes
live near water.
They swim
very well.

Some snakes live
on land. They live
in forests, prairies,
deserts, and cities.

Snakes **slither** when they move. Their bodies curve back and forth to move forward.

A snake smells
with its tongue.
This helps it
hunt frogs, lizards,
mice, **insects**,
and other snakes.

Most snakes do
not chew their food.
They swallow
animals whole.

Snakes open their **jaws** wide. They can eat animals twice their size. Gulp!

21

Glossary

insects—small animals with six legs and hard outer bodies; insect bodies are divided into three parts.

jaws—the bones that form the mouth of an animal

patterns—shapes and designs that repeat; some animals have patterns on their bodies.

scales—hard plates that cover the bodies of some animals

shed—to get rid of the outer layer of skin

slither—to move smoothly across the ground; snakes move their bodies from side to side to slither forward.

To Learn More

AT THE LIBRARY
Patent, Dorothy Hinshaw. *Slinky, Scaly, Slithery Snakes*. New York, N.Y.: Walker & Co., 2000.

Schulte, Mary. *Snakes and Other Reptiles*. New York, N.Y.: Children's Press, 2005.

Thomson, Sarah L. *Amazing Snakes!* New York, N.Y.: HarperCollins Publishers, 2006.

ON THE WEB
Learning more about snakes is as easy as 1, 2, 3.

1. Go to www.factsurfer.com.

2. Enter "snakes" into the search box.

3. Click the "Surf" button and you will see a list of related Web sites.

With factsurfer.com, finding more information is just a click away.

Index

The images in this book are reproduced through the courtesy of: Ra Khalil, front cover; David Chambers, p. 5; Minden Pictures/Masterfile, p. 7; Brent Ward/Alamy, p. 9; Rolf Nussbaumer/Photolibrary, p. 11; John Pitcher/Age Fotostock, p. 13; Juan Martinez, p. 13 (left); Niv Koren, p. 13 (middle); Kushch Dmitry, p. 13 (right); Thomas Shortell, p. 15; Paulo De Oliveira/Photolibrary, p. 17; Arto Hakola, p. 17 (left); Eduard Kyslynskyy, p. 17 (middle); Ew Chee Guan, p. 17 (right); John Cancalosi/Ardea, p. 19; Jack Milchanowski/Alamy, p. 21.